UNDERSTANDING

YOUR 1 YEAR-OLD

UNDERSTANDING

YOUR 1 YEAR-OLD

Deborah Steiner

Warwick Publishing
Toronto Los Angeles

ISBN 1-894020-01-4

Published by:
Warwick Publishing Inc., 388 King Street East, Toronto, Ontario M5V 1K2
Warwick Publishing Inc., 1424 N. Highland Avenue, Los Angeles, CA 90027

Distributed by:
Firefly Books Ltd., 3680 Victoria Park Avenue, Willowdale, Ontario M2H 3K1

First published in Great Britain in 1993 by:
Rosendale Press Ltd.
Premier House
10 Greycoat Place
London SW1P 1SB

Design: Diane Farenick

Printed and bound in Canada

CONTENTS

Tavistock Clinic

The Tavistock Clinic, London, was founded in 1920, in order to meet the needs of people whose lives had been disrupted by the First World War. Today, it is still committed to understanding people's needs though, of course, times and people have changed. Now, as well as working with adults and adolescents, the Tavistock Clinic has a large department for children and families. This offers help to parents who are finding the challenging task of bringing up their children daunting and has, therefore, a wide experience of children of all ages. It is firmly committed to early intervention in the inevitable problems that arise as children grow up, and to the view that if difficulties are caught early enough, parents are the best people to help their children with them.

Professional Staff of the Clinic were, therefore, pleased to be able to contribute to this series of books to describe the ordinary development of children, to help in spotting the growing pains and to provide ways that parents might think about their children's growth.

Introduction

This book is about the 12- to 24-month period of a baby's life, the year which bridges the gap between infancy and childhood. The primary purpose is to offer some understanding about what may lie behind the way the baby is behaving and perhaps give a picture of what it might feel like to be a baby of this age. From 12 to 24 months the baby is learning a great deal, particularly about being a separate person who is able to do more things for himself or herself. Developments are rapid and are often interspersed with periods of rest or regression back to infantile ways. These changes, and how babies and their families manage them, will affect their sense of themselves and help to shape their relationships in the outside world.

In the first year the mother and baby are engaged in the intense business of getting to know each other. If all goes well they manage to find a way of being together, of being in touch with what is needed, at least most of the time. During this period babies depend completely on their mother, with their needs satisfied within the compass of her love and day-to-day care. As tiny infants, however, babies are not aware of dependence on another separate person and Mother is experienced at adapting totally to their needs. From the mother's point of view, as well as feeling gratified at being needed so exclusively, it also sometimes feels as if she is enslaved by "his or her majesty the baby's" incessant demands.

By the time the first birthday comes around, this situation, though basically the same, is slowly changing. In celebrating their child's first birthday, the parents are also congratulating themselves on having steered him or her through the vicissitudes of the first 12 months—an achievement for them and the baby. Thanks to them, the baby now has a firm grip on life, and can get on with the task of growing up. The baby's horizons are widening now to encompass Mother as a separate person, and other members of the family. The baby is more of a person in his or her own right, on the way to becoming a toddler.

The 12- to 24-month period of your child's life is unique in that he or she develops physically at a tremendous rate. For some babies the developments come in leaps and bounds, for others more slowly and steadily. To a child of this age the world is a fascinating place with an infinite variety of secrets to be discovered, and the zest and seriousness with which the baby sets about these discoveries is part of the delight. Your baby has the capacity, long lost to us adults, to find seemingly ordinary things interesting and significant; curiosity and energy seem boundless.

CHAPTER ONE

Milestones; Walking and Talking

Most babies have learned to get around by themselves by the time they reach their first birthday, usually by crawling. For such a baby the next move is to stand upright. But not all babies bother to crawl. One mother reported that her son seemed content to sit around until he managed to stand at about 15 months. He was, however, a great talker! It was as though he was concentrating on that area of development at that point. Jane was a child who never crawled in the conventional way; she had found a curious, but for her effective, method of propelling herself around on her bottom, dragging herself with her left foot. Her mother recalled with some amusement how Jane would scoot down the hall in this awkward way at a great rate when she heard her father's key in the lock. But her parents became increasingly worried as her first birthday came and went and she had still not shown any inclination to stand up. They began to wonder if there was something wrong. Should they take her to a doctor? Should they try to make her stand? Should they wait a bit longer? About a month before her second birthday she suddenly stood up, to her parents' delight and relief. Having made this move, Jane rapidly learned to walk.

Some babies seem to make these advances without much to-do; for others it seems more fraught with difficulty. Ryan went through a very fractious and irritable phase when he had learned to stand but could not bring himself to let go and take a few steps, and his mother had to go through a few weeks of frustration and tension with him. Most parents watch their baby's struggles to stand and walk with a mixture of delight, pride and anxiety. Seeing a child getting to his feet, fall over, then struggle to get up again, one can only be astonished at the grit and determination needed to master this skill, and the frustration that has to be overcome on the way. It is a milestone reached and successfully negotiated, in which parents get very involved, because it is in a way a confirmation and a reward for the hard work they have put in so far. These developmental milestones sometimes come to assume enormous importance for parents. If they are delayed it gives rise to disquiet; if the baby walks and talks early the parents feel proud and secretly triumphant, especially if their baby is quicker than Mrs. Jones's toddler down the road. Some rivalry of this kind is natural but if it becomes excessive it may have more to do with the parents' anxiety about their own successes or failures.

A different view of the world

The world is a very different place to someone who can get around it on his or her own, who can go unaided to another room to fetch another toy, have a look around, or just enjoy the experience of walking. Once upright, the baby's plane of vision changes and hands are now free to do other things. The natural urge to explore, previously confined to his or her own and Mother's body, or to things that were given to him or her, can now be given much wider scope. The baby can get into everything and at a higher level, so that things have to be moved out of reach. Kitchen cupboards, shelves, knobs, handles, switches, drawers—all is suddenly grist to the mill of this boundless curiosity. A child who has just learned to walk, a "junior toddler" as one writer put it, is always on the go, as though driven by a need to practice and perfect this newly acquired skill. Often at this stage babies go through a period of elation when they seem very pleased with themselves and impervious to knocks and falls. There is often a surge of almost omnipotent self-assertiveness, as if now they believe that the world is their oyster. One mother described her daughter at this stage as having "a love affair with the world."

Now on his own two feet, more identified with the adult world and even more able to take command of his own comings and goings our toddler is also psychologically exploring the idea of being more separate from Mother. The outward signs of increasing independence are accompanied by an inner sense of greater certainty about himself, which he wants recognized by his sometimes reluctant parents. This means emotional readjustments, particularly for the mother, who will feel at times a sense of loss and regret that her exclusive relationship with her baby is changing fast. For mothers who found the unique intimacy with their helpless baby particularly gratifying, acceptance of this assertive and self-important toddler can be difficult.

Paradoxically, the sense of greater separateness from Mother brings the infant up against different anxieties. While the baby feels, and is, less helpless, her increasing awareness also makes her realize how much she cannot do; that the world is not her oyster and under her control as she thought it was. It is something of a wound to her self-esteem when she has to face the fact of her smallness and vulnerability, particularly as she becomes more aware that her mother, still the main focus of her world, is independent of her, with her own interests and desires. This makes the child fearful that she will be lost or abandoned, and such fears express themselves in behavior very often seen in junior toddlers. The young toddler will frequently take off from her mother's knee, and venture forth, only to run quickly back to base, as if to get reassurance that Mother is still there, and that she can get back to her. It is remarkable how five or ten minutes of emotional re-charging will revive a flagging infant and enable her to resume her explorations. Another pattern of behavior seen at this stage is the baby running away and not coming back, compelling Mother to run after her. This is often done in the spirit of a game, much enjoyed by the energetic youngster and sometimes enjoyed also by a not-so-energetic mother, but it is also an expression of a need to be reassured that Mother is attentive to her and will not let her get lost. To some extent it is also a testing of the mother's goodwill and acceptance of these tentative bids for freedom. Many babies will, to begin with, only practice their walking if holding onto Mother's finger, as though she is a mere appendage, like a personal "baby-walker!"

Mood swings between independence and clinginess

Spurts of independence and sorties into the wider world are often interspersed with bouts of fretfulness and clinginess, when the baby seems to fall apart and be unable to manage alone. He may for a while be unwilling to let Mother out of sight, as though suddenly frightened of too much freedom, and what he really wants is to be back with Mother as her helpless infant. The baby will trail around after her, hanging on to her skirt, crying to be picked up and reluctant even to let her go to the bathroom without him. In some babies these swings in mood are extreme and very bewildering; other babies seem to go through these developments with relatively little to-do. To some extent this is a matter of temperament. The difficulty for the mother is adjusting to changes in pace. She needs to be able to allow her baby to go at his own rate while judging, often intuitively, when some active encouragement would help the child over a timid period, or when to put a few brakes on if he seems to be over-reaching himself. Sometimes the baby at this stage seems not to know quite what he wants—to be allowed his freedom or to be held on to. Ryan's mother reported a short period when he would cry and whine to be picked up but as soon as she put him on her knee he would cry to be put down. He seemed to want to be able to leave Mother but at the same time not sure that he should.

Many mothers are very worried when their one year-old seems to lose her grip and revert to babyishness, as though they fear she will never make it and become independent. It helps to remember that the independence of this age is only relative; the forays into the adult world are not yet secure and your one year-old is a small baby still, and very much in need of Mother's physical and emotional availability.

Talking

From the very first day of life, communication is going on between a mother and her baby. The mother does this with her touch, her eyes and her voice. The mother's physical care of her baby, the way she handles him, is also a psychological experience for the baby; through her care for his physical needs the mother is also expressing her feelings for him. Mothers tend instinctively to talk to their infants, not only because that is an adult's natural way of communicating, but also because her voice can span a distance. Thus, when she is not actually holding the baby, her voice will provide a "holding" sensation for him. For instance Mother's talking will often take the form of putting into words how the baby might be feeling at that moment or putting a name to whatever the baby seems to be gazing at. Some mothers use their voice in this way more than others, but some talking to the infant in the course of her daily care of him is vital if he is to become accustomed to sounds and later, words.

In early infancy the baby is also communicating with Mother with the same senses but in a different way. Her baby will gaze at her perhaps while feeding; when she talks to him he will wave his arms around or seem to strain to move towards her. The baby will turn his head towards her breast, aware of her warmth and smell, and his eager sucking and touching her clothes or breast will communicate pleasure at her closeness. But of course the most important and urgent way he gets through to his mother is by his cries and screams when in distress or pain, and mothers are quick to learn, sometimes intuitively, sometimes by trial and error, the different cries of their infant.

The importance of talking to your baby

Towards the end of the first year, as the baby is becoming more separate, more complex sounds will emerge, more like words copying the words Mother says. The ability to do this springs directly from a natural urge to make contact but also from the experience of hearing Mother talk. At first the baby revels in making the sounds which Mother will repeat back, helping to define them more clearly. First sounds are usually Mama or Dada and Baba, and later on the important word "no" will appear. Mama, Dada and Baba, the most significant words for the baby, seem to derive from sounds the baby is already making naturally. The words your toddler then goes on to learn vary according to experiences and the interests of the family. The age for the baby's first word, and the rate at which he continues to learn to talk, vary tremendously from one baby to another. One child may accumulate a large vocabulary early, while another may be interested in what is going on around but be reluctant to give up babyish ways of communicating. If your baby is generally alert and interested in surroundings, there is no need to worry if actual words are slow in coming at this stage.

The one year-old gradually learns to ask for things, to indicate wants by means of words rather than signals or gestures, but at first the two come together and the words form only part of the total communication. Often the situation itself is self-explanatory, or the mother's tone of voice is enough without actual words being distinguished. In this way the mother is teaching her infant how to speak ,and out of these unmistakable situations the child picks out and learns the appropriate words. The mother, in talking to her baby, needs to use one word or phrase often, talking simply and clearly; but she must also talk in sentences, otherwise her infant will have a bleak and disconnected experience of words. Again, this is something most mothers do very early on even though they know the infant cannot understand the actual words. She will tell her baby what she is doing as she prepares their food, or where they are going as she gets him ready, and what will happen when they get home. Hearing the words from Mother in this way accustoms the baby to sounds and words in the context of a good feeling of security and being included. It also adds to the richness of his experience to hear the tones and cadences of the mother's voice; later on he will draw on this experience when making sentences; it can in fact be very revealing to hear one's child speaking in a voice so clearly one's own!

Nursery rhymes and lap- or finger-games like "Itsy, Bitsy Spider" and "This Little Piggy" are invaluable, as well as being greatly enjoyed. The baby becomes familiar with words through constant repetition, and in the context of pleasurable close physical contact with Mother or Father.

As talking develops so does the power of reasoning, of being able to make connections, of anticipating the next move. At 18 months, Michael loved to be taken by his grandmother to stand and watch trains passing on the nearby railway. Before a train had come he would say, half as a question, half as a demand, "More trains are coming." He had developed a capacity to remember previous visits and was able to associate seeing the tracks with the trains coming. The tone of his voice was very rich, suggesting his excited impatience and anticipation; saying the words in this way also seemed to help him to endure the waiting, never easy for a small child.

The importance of listening to your baby

This brings us to one of the most important factors in the baby's learning to talk. A baby cannot just take in language by himself from an adult environment. The other half of the process is the mother and other members of the family talking to the baby and listening to his response. Babies in institutions who do not have an interested mother or mother-substitute devoting time and attention to their babbles and later their words have a sparse and limited vocabulary. Children in large families may also be slow to speak; although there may be a lot of talking going on, there may be no one person taking the time to talk and listen quietly to what a child of this age is trying to say. The infant's attempts to make himself understood get lost in the general hubbub. There is often a tendency too in large families where there are older brothers and sisters for the baby's demands to be anticipated too quickly before the child has a chance to struggle to get the right words out.

Sitting down quietly to look at a picture book with the baby, say at bedtime, is one of the best ways of helping the child's understanding of words while also enriching his experience. The baby will at first enjoy hearing Mother or Father talk about the pictures and will be encouraged in this way to begin to say the words himself. To be able to look at a representation of a cup, say, to imagine it and think about it, is a major intellectual advance for a baby of this age from being an infant who can only take into his mind what is actually there in front of him. Being on Mother's knee, or in close proximity to her or with Father at the end of a tiring day, comforts the baby, and associates learning with a sense of shared pleasure and security.

CHAPTER TWO

Your One Year-Old And The Family

In the first chapter I talked about your one year-old's increasing mastery of her body and capacity to explore the physical environment. Beginning to use words also enables your child to take a more active and assertive role in the interactions that are going on around her. The kind of relationships she is making at this stage are deeply rooted in, and influenced by, the early relationship with Mother and from this will come her inner feelings about herself as a person.

Responding to increasing independence

Mothers have different reactions to their infants striking out for themselves. Most feel a sense of relief that their once utterly dependent infant is now more robust and able to manage on his own to some extent at least. Some are more conservative and slow to adapt to their baby's growing individuality. Others have so enjoyed the experience of having a tiny infant dependent on them alone that they are sorry to give it up, and secretly resent the baby no longer needing them so exclusively. The close physical intimacy with a new baby is for other mothers an uncomfortable experience; for them bottle feeding, for example, feels preferable and they will feel eager to have the baby on his own two feet, taking solid food and feeding himself. Such a mother may come into her own when the baby is more independent. In fact the majority of mothers will recognize all these states of mind as familiar at one time or another. Circumstances may play a part in this as will the mother's personality derived in turn from her own early experiences. Usually delight and pride in the baby's rapid developments at this stage are mixed with feelings of sadness and loss when the uniqueness of the relationship between Mother and newborn has to be relinquished.

Your one year-old 's burgeoning awareness that Mother has interests and concerns of her own independent of him deals something of a blow to him and considerable tact and sensitivity are needed to help him to come to terms with the knowledge that he is not the sole focus of her world. Help with the pain of having to face this unwelcome reality, will also encourage him to find solace in other relationships and spur him on to explore and widen his experiences with others. Other adults and brothers and sisters become important to the baby during this period and as his world enlarges Father becomes an increasingly significant figure, both in his own right and as someone who has his own particular relationship with the baby's mother.

From very early on there is a difference in the way the baby behaves towards each parent. The emotions between the infant and mother run very deep and are sometimes painful. The baby is dependent on Mother in a way that he is not on Father. The experience of a father who leaves in the morning and comes back in the evening allows the baby to learn about separations in the context of a relationship which is less intense, though Father's absences may nevertheless be keenly felt. Father's reappearance at the end of the day is often a special event, and felt to some extent to be a welcome escape from the intensity of the relationship with Mother. As well as having loving feelings towards Mother, the baby has angry feelings, especially when she thwarts or frustrates him, and it can be quite a relief for mother and baby after a long and tiring day together when Father returns. Father returning, may also be able to intervene to break a deadlock or resolve a battle, say with feeding, which mother and baby have got themselves into. If Father is not around, another adult, like a grandparent or close friend who is familiar with the baby, may be able from time to time to step in and give Mother a rest from the strains of being with her toddler all day.

Mixed feelings towards Father

However, the baby's feelings towards Father are also mixed, and this is true of both boys and girls. The one year-old is more able to comprehend the parents as a couple, and this is not an altogether welcome idea. When the parents are perceived having a friendly and mutually supportive relationship, the baby undoubtedly feels secure and reassured. Your baby also, rightly, wants sometimes to be included in this. When Father comes home and the parents talk together he wants to join in, particularly if he has learned some new word, or made a new discovery. This is part of his natural desire to be seen now as an individual member of the family. But again the child's feelings are mixed. The parents' relationship arouses anger and jealousy so that the baby also wants to keep them separate. He may be reluctant to go to bed in the evening, or he may turn up in between them in the middle of the night and be reluctant to go back to his own bed. Now he is mobile he can make his presence felt in this way. In the daytime his "joining in" may also contain the wish to stop them being together. When Michael at 23 months would shout furiously "no talk" and bang loudly on the tray of his high chair he was making it very clear that he found his parents' interest in each other very hard to bear. The different responses of boys and girls to each parent become more marked during this year. For the boy Father is a much admired figure whom he wants to copy and identify with. However the baby boy is still very much bound up with intensely possessive feelings for his mother so that Father sometimes seems to him like a huge and threatening rival, who will take Mother away, and be angry with his son when he wants Mother to himself. The girl, like her brother, is also intensely involved in her relationship with her mother and is beginning to identify with her. Her wish to have a special and close relationship with her father makes her feel rivalrous with her mother, on whom she still depends. Girls often become very cuddly and flirtatious towards their fathers, to the extent of making Mother sometimes feel hurt and pushed out. The baby's preference for one parent or the other can be so obvious at times that it becomes difficult for parents to handle their own feelings, particularly at times when they are quarreling or feeling angry with one another.

At this age both boys and girls often seem to become more upset by Father's anger or disapproval than Mother's. This happened to Anna when she was about 20 months old. When her father's key was heard in the front door, she rushed excitedly to meet him. He had picked up some groceries and Anna demanded to carry a jar of jelly in to the kitchen. In her excitement she dropped it on the floor where it smashed, sending jelly and glass everywhere. Her father, feeling momentarily exasperated, spoke to her very sharply, whereupon Anna seemed to crumple. She burst into desolate sobs and ran to her mother who picked her up and comforted her. It was some time before she was consoled and could get back to friendly relations with her father. It seemed as though her desperate wish to please him and show off to him how clever she was had ended in failure and this was too much for her to bear.

The only child and brothers and sisters

The one year-old who is the first or only child enjoys a special relationship with the parents. He or she has their love and attention without having to share it with other children in the family. But it can be a great strain on an only child to have to focus all the intensity of his emotions on his two parents, and indeed to have them investing their attention and expectations on him alone. Being a younger child means never having the luxury of the specialness of the first or only child, and having to compete from the start for Mother's attention. What a younger child gains is in being at once part of the hustle and bustle of a family with its already existing network of relationships. The baby spends much of his time watching the comings and goings of his brothers and sisters, now puzzled, now admiring, now wary. How the baby gets along with them depends of course on the personalities of all the children concerned, but an important variable is the age gap.

Elizabeth had an older sister, Ann, aged 5 and a brother, Charlie, aged 6½ who were very close. Elizabeth's birth was anticipated with great excitement and trepidation by Ann and Charlie and they were pleased and relieved when she arrived safe and sound. Both the older children found comfort and companionship in each other, as though being together helped them to cope with feeling left out when their mother was preoccupied with the baby. While the baby was tiny and sleeping most of the time they could comfortably ignore her; the problems began to escalate when she became a toddler and more of a force to be reckoned with.

The increasing skills of a younger sibling pose problems for older children who are close in age and not long out of babyhood themselves. There will undoubtedly be times when a 3 year-old will be genuinely delighted with the progress of his toddler brother or sister, but sometimes he will also feel that his own uncertain sense of being grown up is threatened. William was just three when his brother James was 14 months. James was sitting on the floor in the living room with William while his mother was in the kitchen making coffee for a neighbor. William began to play a game with a paper model of a black bat, which he flew around and around in the air. James watched this intently and gurgled delightedly. William flew the bat nearer and nearer to James until it was hitting his head, making James blink. William then wrapped it around James's head, pulling it tightly and covering James's eyes. James whimpered at first then cried more loudly. William then picked James up saying, "I can pick you up," but then sat him down hard on the floor. Mother then came into the room to see what was going on and to rescue James.

As Mother was talking to her visitor later James was pulling himself up on the coffee table. William lay down near him, pulled him back into a sitting position and then pushed him over onto his side. The mother did not see this happen and when she went over to see why James was crying William said the baby had banged his head! We can see here how William was jealous on two counts—his mother was talking to her friend, and James was beginning to grow up and do things for himself. He seems to try hard to "mother" James when he picks him up, but his jealousy gets the better of him again and he sits James down heavily. Also it seems as though William would dearly like to be the baby instead of James so that his mother would pick him up and cuddle him. James, for his part, is both enraptured by the doings of his big brother and also a little scared of him.

There are occasions when older children have to be protected from the depredations of their jealous or angry baby sibling. Zoe's mother recalled an occasion when a friend came over for coffee and Zoe, aged 20 months was upstairs, being rather quiet. She was found in her older sister's bedroom silently cutting through a photograph of her sister which she had found on the dressing table. Zoe, it seemed had not taken kindly to seeing her sister going away that morning with her grandmother for a holiday! Her mother gently remonstrated with Zoe and, sensing that she was jealous and hurt, cuddled her while she taped the photo together.

A new pregnancy

By the time their child is in the second year of life, parents may begin to think of having another baby. A child of this age, with increasing awareness of the people around him, will quickly sense, even when the mother's pregnancy is not obvious, that she is absorbed in something else. It may be just an undefined feeling that something is up. As time goes on there will be literally less room on mother's lap, and the toddler will begin to feel ousted even before the baby is born. When the toddler is feeling particularly angry or hurt by Mother's new pregnancy, his father, or perhaps a loved grandparent, will be a source of comfort and reassurance. He will be greatly helped also if the parents recognize his hurt and talk about it, and allow him to express some of his feelings. Sometimes parents find the intensity of their toddler's anger and jealousy very startling for instance he may try to hit his mother's stomach, or destroy a favorite toy. Sleeping troubles, eating difficulties, temper tantrums or a set-back in toilet training may occur around this time—in such ways the one year-old expresses deeply felt emotions about a disturbing event like a pregnancy in the family. Talking about the coming birth in terms that he can understand and particularly about the arrangements to look after him when his mother is hospitalized, will help him to feel included in the event, and reassure him that he has a secure place in the family despite the new baby.

Looking after toddler and infant

Looking after an infant and a toddler requires considerable organization. This is particularly so at feeding times during the day, when the mother has to find a way of giving the baby a reasonably quiet feed, while keeping an eye on her errant toddler. Michael's mother was at her wits end during a period when Michael was finding it almost too much to see his sister being breast fed. As she settled down to feed her Michael would somehow get himself into mischief which meant that his mother had to get up to rescue him. Sometimes he could be pacified with having a bottle at the same time but his mother could relax more when she hit on the idea of having Michael in the playpen close to her knees while she fed the baby so that he could reach out and touch her and she him. Another mother solved the problem by having the older child on her other knee, and reading while the infant was feeding.

Reactions to being left

Contrary to much popular myth, even very young babies are sensitive to what is going on around them, but by the second year they are intellectually more able to make connections between things or events. An example would be when Jane aged 15 months would rush to the fridge when her mother brought milk home from the store, knowing that was where it was kept. A combination of a babysitter arriving and Mother putting on lipstick will quickly signify to our observant one year-old that Mother is going out—he may have already got wind of it in some other less obvious way such as Mother's increased haste, or preoccupied manner as she prepares the food. Different babies react in different ways to their mother leaving them. One will immediately cry and cling to her, pushing the babysitter away, even if it is a known and loved person like Father or grandmother; another will seem not to notice much but be very fractious when Mother returns. Ryan's mother left him at 20 months with his father playing in the garden for an hour while she went out shopping. He played happily clambering on the big stones his father was using to make a rock garden. Mother returned, and as Ryan saw her he fell from a height of 6 inches and bellowed loudly, so that his mother, who could see that he was emotionally rather than physically hurt, picked him up and cuddled him.

Sometimes, especially after a longish separation, a child of this age will withdraw coldly from Mother on her return and he may need coaxing back to friendly relations, as though he needs to reject her as he feels she has rejected him with her going away. A very common experience mothers have at this age, but also later, is of the baby kicking up an enormous fuss at the prospect of Mother going out, but then settling down well once she has gone. Such a baby seems to need his mother to take the upset on board and carry it for him. Slipping out, hoping the child won't notice, is usually a mistake. Such a tactic may relieve the mother of the immediate pain of having to disappoint and anger her baby, but in the long run such deception, if done constantly, will undermine his trust and make him feel insecure. He may well then react by becoming very clingy lest he be suddenly abandoned. Having assured herself that the baby is fed, comfortable and in good hands, the mother can help the baby cope better with the separation by a confident and affectionate goodbye. As the child gets older and can understand more, a brief explanation of where she is going and when she will be back will help him settle down.

The value of brief separations

From time to time it is good for both mother and child to be away from each other for a while. Being with a toddler all day is tiring and tedious and mothers need the respite of adult company. Getting away from an ever-demanding baby means Mother can come back refreshed. For the child it can also be relief to know that his jealous possessiveness does not actually stop his mother doing things she wants to do for herself. Having to manage for a while without his mother will encourage the toddler to deepen other relationships, say with Father and brothers and sisters or with other children; a regular substitute carer can enrich the child's world, as long as Mother is around.

Parents naturally want their child to grow up to be independent, but sometimes parents become so eager for this that they expect more than the child can manage. There is a risk then of calling it being independent when the baby seems never to notice when Mother leaves or returns and doesn't react in any way. It is important to remember that it is healthy and right for a child to protest when his mother leaves him. He is showing that she matters to him, and persistent indifference to her absence or presence would be a cause for concern.

Going into hospital

Longer separations are sometimes unavoidable, for example if the child has to spend time in the hospital. Children's wards in hospital these days are increasingly organized around the childrens' needs. They are often bright and cheerfully decorated, with plenty of toys and specially trained staff. Provision is normally made for mothers to stay with their baby—a far cry from the days not so long ago, when parents were told to hand over the child at the entrance so that she would not be upset. In fact research has shown that children recover more quickly if their mothers can look after them at least some of the time.

Nevertheless, going into hospital is still a bewildering experience for a small child, as indeed it can be for adults. Children of this age should always be taken in and settled by Mother or Father, or if that isn't possible, by another known and trusted adult. Older toddlers will be greatly helped by an explanation, given in simple language, of where they are going and what will happen to them. For younger children, whose grasp of words is more limited, being talked to about what is happening will give them a sense that their fears are recognized and understood. Hospitals and doctors can be intimidating places where parents may feel overwhelmed by professional expertise but it is worth making a great effort to be with your baby as much as is feasible. It is also important not to be satisfied with well-meaning assurances that a child of this age doesn't really understand and therefore won't be frightened. An ordinary alert one year-old who doesn't miss a trick is hardly likely to become blank and unaware of being in a totally strange environment.

If there are other children in the family it is not always possible for the mother to be with the child in hospital all the time; Father or a grandparent may be able to step in here, or perhaps a neighbor, to look after the other children. If the baby is staying in for more than a few days it may be possible for the other children to be brought on occasions to visit; this will give a reassuring sense to the hospitalized child of being thought of as an important member of the family and his capacity to cope with a frightening situation will be strengthened.

If frequent short visits are all that can be managed by Mother the child will at least be reassured that he has not been forgotten, but he may cry bitterly when Mother or Father has to leave. This is very distressing but is actually a good sign that the child still feels very much a part of the relationship with his parents; it helps the child to be able to express being upset and feel his mother can bear it with him.

Mothers returning to work

By the time the baby reaches this age many mothers are thinking of going back to work. Whether this is because of financial necessity or because the mother wants to resume her working life it is really a question of finding the best way of doing it, bearing her own and the baby's needs in mind. How the child copes with the separation will depend partly on temperament and partly on the relationship already established with mother. Jane, the baby mentioned earlier who was slow to stand up, continued throughout childhood to find separations very hard to bear, even though generally she was a lively, happy child who had a good relationship with her mother. Much can be done to help the child to cope with separation and even to profit from the chance to make other meaningful relationships. Being left in the care of someone known and trusted, preferably in their own home with familiar things around them is essential and will also put Mother's mind at ease. It would be even better if the baby can be looked after together with a brother or sister, or another child. But however good the arrangements it is normal for a small child to show some disturbance when there is a major change in her life, such as Mother going back to work. Mrs. Shepherd went back to work when her first child Alison was a year-old. She had already found a babysitter who had looked after Alison during her first year from time to time, so that they had already established a good relationship. A few weeks after Mother started work, Alison went through a period lasting several weeks when she would not take any food from her mother, but she ate normally with the sitter, who would exclaim what a good appetite Alison had! Of course this was in a way reassuring for Mrs. Shepherd to know that Alison was happy and eating well while she was at work, but it was also painful for her to have to bear the child's temporary rejection of her.

While a certain amount of separation from Mother is necessary and even beneficial, parents should not expect too much independence of a baby of this age. A one year-old is still very much in need of Mother as an anchor and source of comfort. There may be very long periods when he or she can be self-sufficient and manage without Mother but there will inevitably be times when the baby's hard-won confidence deserts him and he reverts back to baby-like behavior.

This happened to Zoe, at 23 months, when her mother began to leave her for a few hours a day in a small independent daycare center. Zoe's mother, and the mothers managing the daycare were astonished when she seemed from the first day to allow her mother to leave her without a cry or a whimper. However, Zoe seemed to express her anxiety about being left by clinging doggedly to her lunch box for the whole time she was at the there—she would not let go of it for a second. Only when she got home would she drop it and forget it. After about a month Zoe became much more clinging and distressed when her mother left, as though being so grown-up had become too much for her.

Being a single parent

So far we have been talking about the relationships of the one year-old in the context of a family where there are two parents to share the task of bringing up the children. Nowadays it is not unusual for one parent to be bringing up children, usually the mother, but sometimes the father. In the next chapter I will be talking about some of the typical problems and issues that arise with children of this age, which can make parents feel especially anxious and helpless. Dealing with them alone, especially sleeping and eating difficulties, is particularly stressful for a single parent. Without some kind of external help and support, say from sympathetic grandparents or a friendly neighborhood network, the strain may sometimes feel intolerable. Financial necessity also often means the mother must work at least part-time to make ends meet, bringing the added burden of finding good childcare. Making contact with other mothers with whom worries and anxieties can be shared and ideas swapped about how to cope will go some way towards easing the stress and often the isolation of being with a toddler. Public health employees or social workers and family doctors are in a good position to give information about local parent groups and activities which will benefit both mother and baby.

CHAPTER THREE

Your One Year-Old And Everyday Life

The conflicts and stresses which are part and parcel of the baby's drive to become his own person, affect all aspects of his daily life. We have seen how his more independent feelings about himself exhilarate and frighten him, and how his forays into the adult world, marked by periods of triumphant assertiveness and lapses into babyishness, are now making different demands on his parents.

By the time your baby reaches her first birthday, her daily routine will have changed considerably and will probably be more in rhythm with the rest of the family. Sleeping and eating, however, still make up a major part of life, with playing becoming an increasingly important activity. Regular routine gives the baby a sense of order and predictability, with the reassurance that things are continuous and not forgotten. But the developmental path never runs smoothly and in the course of daily life there are an infinite number of vicissitudes and upsets, some obvious, others not, which disturb your one year-old. This chapter deals with some of the most common problems that occur during this period of the child's life.

Sleeping patterns

As adults, we are all familiar with bouts of sleeplessness, usually when there is something on our mind, some unresolved problem or anxiety perhaps that we are barely conscious of. Babies and children are equally prey to such troubles which frequently give rise to sleep disturbances and nightmares, with the added complication for small infants that they have not the verbal capacity to express their fears, even to themselves. If a child has a nightmare, it may make him nervous about going to sleep on subsequent nights. A father was asked how his two year-old was and he replied, "she's lovely but she has an annoying habit of waking up in the night and calling out. She settles immediately after one of us has gone in and given her a cuddle but we don't know why she is doing it." He thought on the first occasion she did this that she had a dream but now he wondered if it had become a habit. The truth is that we often do not know why a child suddenly starts waking in the night. Perhaps for the little girl above, it had become a habit which would need a little firmness to stop. Anna's mother reported something similar: Anna would be satisfied if, when she woke in the night she just had a glimpse of her mother, she would then go to sleep lying on top of her bottle which she always took to bed with her, as though to make sure no one would take it away. This is a form of separation anxiety, where the child is frightened of being away from her mother and the familiar daytime world.

Infants differ constitutionally in the amount of sleep they need—this seems to be a fact of life. Even children within the same family show marked differences in their sleep patterns and needs. A tense, colicky infant is less likely to be able to let go and fall asleep than a more placid one. Similarly some babies sleep more heavily than others, and are less disturbed by noise. The mother's personality also plays a part, for if a mother feels overly anxious, this will transmit as a general tension to the baby and make falling asleep more difficult.

The average one year-old will be moving towards a routine which will include an afternoon nap and a longer period of sleep at night. Throughout this year, however, many infants will be waking up for a late-night feed around midnight, maybe more for comfort than actual hunger. Many mothers also are loath to give up this feed as it is often the quietest and most undisturbed and a time when some of the lost closeness of early infancy can be recaptured. The constancy of this feed may be important to the mother and the baby at this stage when many changes in development and daily routine are taking place.

Sleep disturbance manifests itself in various ways. The baby may be unwilling to be put to bed; he may be unable to fall asleep; or he may go to sleep only to wake several times during the night. Bedtime for babies at this age is usually around 7 PM, perhaps when Father is already home and can put the child to bed or read a story, giving Mother a break.

There is often a lot going on in a household at this time, especially if there are older children, and a meal is being prepared. Add to this the tiredness from practicing walking, investigating, exploring, being with other children perhaps, and it is easy to see how difficult it might be to give all this up and leave the stage to others. It means not only giving up the stage, but giving up Mother to Father and the other children.

The value of bedtime rituals

Familiar bedtime rituals will help to calm down an over-excited baby. A series of events which the baby knows lead up to being put into bed gives him a sense of control over what happens to him, as will a quiet review of what happened during the day and what is going to happen tomorrow. One mother of 23-month-old twins, for whom bath- and bedtime was always a bit of a scramble, was helped by her babies who took turns to get into the tub first, and knew each day whose turn it was.

However gently and lovingly put to bed, it can feel like a lonely place, and children of this age characteristically take all sorts of things into their crib with them. They may have to be arranged in a certain way, each toy having its own place in the crib. Being put to bed is a separation, for mother and baby, and in having familiar toys with him the baby is learning to cope with feelings of loneliness and being left out. He may also be identifying with his mother, putting all his family to bed.

Michael had a teddy bear and a panda—the teddy was hugged tightly, in a sort of stranglehold, while Michael sucked his thumb getting ready for sleep; the panda had to be in the corner of the crib, near to Michael's head, as though on guard! There was a period too, at around 18 months when Michael liked to have the curtains open so that he could see the street light, and the closet door shut. Jane was unable to go to sleep without her blanket to which she had become very attached during her first year. She would hug it to her face when put into her crib, then with two fingers in her mouth, and stroking the corner of the blanket gently across her cheek, she would gradually fall asleep. Zoe's bedtime toy was a rabbit; she was a child who seemed to roam around her crib before collapsing into sleep in some curious position, but always on her stomach, on top of her rabbit.

Many children, at this age, become very attached to a particularly object—either a toy, or blanket, or a scarf belonging to Mother and this attachment can be so strong that the child feels incomplete without it. It may have to go everywhere with the child, or be only needed at night. With it close by the toddler feels protected from being sad or lonely—it is like having a part of Mother there giving a sense of inner security. Thumb-sucking, which many mothers feel disturbed by, though needlessly, serves a similar purpose of filling a space, giving the child something of his own to hang on to, and perhaps recalling to the infant the longed-for breast or bottle.

Trying to understand and cope with sleep disturbance

Any change in the child's life may trigger some sort of sleep disturbance. Being away from home, for instance, where he has to sleep in a strange crib; or Mother going back to work and being therefore less available to him; or a new baby in the family. Such changes and upheavals remind him painfully of how dependent and vulnerable he is, and stir up anxieties, never far away for a one year-old, of being lost or forgotten. Anxious wakefulness as mentioned before, can become a habit—Jane at 15 months had a bad cold which made it difficult for her to breathe and she would wake several times during the night fretful and miserable. Her mother duly went in to comfort her, but after a while it seemed that Jane, now much better, rather liked the idea of her mother running in when she called and was now using it to control her. Her mother had finally to be very firm, say a final goodnight and let Jane cry herself to sleep. As the infant is becoming more aware of his parents as a couple, calling out at night or creeping into their bed may be the baby's attempt to keep his parents apart because he feels jealous and left out. It is terribly important to recognize that the baby has such feelings, but he will feel more secure if he feels his parents can say no to him when he tries to invade their privacy. On occasions such as these it may be easier for Father to provide a firm hand.

Perhaps the truly difficult thing about being the parent of a baby who can't sleep is not knowing what is wrong, what is making the baby so restless and wakeful, and having to try and find ways of coping. Stories abound of desperate parents walking the stroller around the block at midnight or going for car rides in the small hours experiencing agony and despair when the baby wakes yet again at the traffic lights, or when Father is trying ever so gently to transfer him from car to crib. Walking and rocking the baby sometimes helps and is made easier if there are two parents to share the strain. It is hard to feel endlessly patient and loving towards a screaming baby who can't be comforted, particularly at 2 AM. Night after night it becomes impossible and ways may have to be found to enable the mother to get some rest.

One mother remembered vividly her feelings of helplessness and mounting fury as she walked around unable to stop the baby's cries and how thankful she was that her husband could take over when she was getting dangerously angry with the baby. For a single parent it can be even more nightmarish; practical steps may actually be vital here—like arranging some help from another adult so that the mother (or father) can get some sleep. Parents may sometimes resort to bringing the baby into bed with them, often in a desperate bid to get some sleep themselves, and this may work but it does bring with it another problem of persuading the child to go back to his own crib later on.

There is nothing more wearing than having to cope with the stresses and strains of the day without a decent night's sleep; and the cumulative effect of weeks or even months of broken nights is truly devastating. Perhaps some comfort can be drawn from knowing that it probably won't go on forever and that it is a problem all parents experience. Talking about it with other parents may help relieve the anxiety and despair.

Feeding: the core of the mother/infant relationship

From the very first day of his life, the nature of the baby's relationship to his mother is centered around feeding, and to a large extent this is still true for the one year-old, even though the routine and kind of food he is eating have changed. It is also true to say that the mother's sense of identity as a mother, and her wish to be a good mother who can provide nourishment for her infant is also focused around the food she offers. The preparation and giving of food is a demonstration of her love for her baby—in a way she is offering part of herself as she did when she offered the breast or bottle to the tiny infant. When the baby is hungry and takes her food eagerly the mother feels pleased and derives confirmation that she is doing all right as a mother. When the baby is not hungry, is uninterested or pushes food away the mother has to bear not just the anxiety of why the baby is not eating but also at a deeper level a sense of being rejected herself. Later on in this section I will describe in detail the particular, but very common, difficulties one mother and baby got into over feeding.

Worries about whether the baby is getting enough to eat run very deep; they spring to some extent from having the awesome responsibility for the life of another person. Having a baby refuse to eat, or eating very little makes the mother anxious that the baby will become ill or even starve. Actually it is very, very rare for a baby to starve itself—babies cling tenaciously to life and can thrive on what may seem to an adult a ridiculously small amount of food. The average one year-old will be having three meals a day, a mixture of solid food and milk, with perhaps a bottle or breast feed early in the morning and late at night.

But what is the average baby? Children vary enormously in the amount they eat, not only as individuals but from week to week or month to month. A bout of teething or a minor illness can put a baby off food for several days. When Michael had the flu at 18 months he refused everything except banana and milk with a few crackers for a week. A change in routine or a family upheaval can have the same effect. At the age of 21 months Jane was left together with her older brother in the care of her aunt and her family, with whom Jane was very familiar, while her parents went away for a week. She refused to eat anything solid for the whole week, causing considerable anxiety to her aunt. Her aunt sensed that this was Jane's way of protesting about her mother leaving her, and did not force her to eat. Jane lost some weight but soon made it up when she was back in her familiar routine. Some children will eat almost nothing outside the house, whereas others who have been poor eaters at home may be encouraged by eating with other people. Sitting alone with mother anxiously hovering over her may result in the child having difficulty eating because she senses mother's anxiety.

Food fads

It is not unusual for children at this stage to have intense likes and dislikes about food. Sometimes this has the quality of a fad, that is eating a particular food almost exclusively for a while then suddenly for no apparent reason, rejecting it and going on to something else. The baby needs to have these preferences respected by Mother even if they seem like fads. At this point in development when a toddler is establishing her own identity, she needs to be given the freedom to make a statement about herself like, this week I am a person who likes apple but not carrot.

Like adults children do develop real aversions to certain tastes or textures and these should be respected. Jane took an instant dislike to fish when she was first offered it, and continued to dislike it throughout childhood. Jane, like many babies of this age, was now exploring the possibility of a more separate relationship with her mother with the added dimension of her wish to control what she did and did not take in; what she ate and in what form. She was learning to discriminate. One baby may reject sloppy baby foods and only like dry firm food that can be held, while another may insist on mushy baby food. By offering both at different times the mother can give her baby the chance to decide and choose for herself.

One of the most common and difficult problems that arises in children of this age is the sudden and persistent refusal of food, particularly solid food. Constant rejection of food carefully prepared is very hard to bear and can provoke strong feelings of helplessness, resentment and anger in the mother towards her rebellious baby. It is an area where mothers and babies can become locked in a battle of wills, with Mother becoming increasingly angry and even demoralized and the baby becoming more determined not to eat. In this situation the baby seems often only to want the bottle or breast and this in itself arouses mother's anxiety that her baby is not growing up at all, but rather insisting on staying a baby. It also begins to feel as though the baby is using a newly found assertiveness to tyrannize and deliberately thwart mother. Mealtimes, instead of being pleasurable occasions, become embattled affairs, fraught with tension and anxiety. When this happens, as it invariably does from time to time, it may need another person to step in and help, someone like Father or a grandparent, who is not so embroiled.

Not knowing why this is happening, together with an awful feeling that the baby is going backwards not forwards or may not be getting the right nutrition, leads to angry confrontations like, "You're not getting out of that chair until you've eaten those peas!" It may help at such a moment to ask if it really matters whether he or she eats "those peas." And if he is demanding the bottle before he takes anything else, is there a good reason why he shouldn't have it this way? Something may have happened which has caused the baby to go back to wanting this symbol of his babyhood.

Michael began to demand his bottle once more soon after his sister was born, even though he had been quite content beforehand with his lidded cup. In this way he was expressing in the only way he could, his jealousy of the baby and his wish to regain what he had lost not so long ago. Children of this age are by nature interested in being grown up but they are still babies and they need to feel that they will still be accepted as such. Being the parent of a one year-old requires a good measure of sensitivity as to when to let your child go at his own pace, even if it sometimes seems like going backwards, and when to encourage him to progress further in his attempts to be grown up.

When the stubborn one year-old is refusing to eat what Mother has prepared, she may have the difficult task of swallowing her pride and giving in gracefully, either by trying to find something her baby will eat, or leaving it to try again at the next mealtime. The baby may indeed be flexing his muscles and a wise mother will go along with this, while using her ingenuity to ensure that the baby is getting a reasonably healthy diet. It sometimes helps to go over what the baby has actually eaten in the course of the day—it may seem odd as a diet but nevertheless be quite adequate to see the baby through. A more difficult question the mother may need to ask herself is whether she is confronting the baby head-on over food, because she is finding the baby's assertiveness too much of a challenge to her authority, or resenting this desire to say no to her and take more control. It is very disturbing when a one year-old in this way makes the parents feel entirely impotent and it requires considerable strength of mind not to be drawn into a battle to prove that you are bigger and stronger than your toddler.

Getting a child to feed himself also means coming up against his mixed feelings about doing things for himself. Your baby is both naturally eager to be grown up but also loath to give up the specialness of being a baby, of being fed. This is often an issue if there is a younger baby in the family. When the baby does want to feed himself, some mothers find it more difficult to accept and encourage than others. A certain amount of mess is inevitable and practical measures like feeding the baby in the kitchen where mess can be cleaned up easily will lessen mother's anxiety on that score.

To learn this new skill, the baby must of necessity resist his mother's attempts to feed him. Your baby also needs to have the chance to explore and finger his food, to feel its texture. For a lively, inquisitive one year-old having a plateful of mashed potatoes or ground beef put in front of him is an opportunity not to be missed and he will prod, squeeze and maybe try and get some of it into his mouth. Some gritting of the teeth on mother's part is necessary here, and perhaps some judicious using of the spoon herself while he is busy. Learning to use a spoon is literally a hit and miss affair to begin with, but with the right encouragement your baby will enjoy it enormously.

I would like now to describe in more detail the kind of difficulties Mrs. Martin got into with Anna, and I have chosen this example because it is a very common kind of situation that mothers find themselves in with infants of this age.

From the start Anna was a difficult baby to feed. She was slow to suckle and easily distracted so that the feeds took a very long time. In addition she sucked up what seemed to her mother a lot of milk after each feed. Nevertheless she thrived and put on weight though she was never a big baby. Mrs. Martin was constantly anxious about whether Anna was getting enough to eat; she breast fed her for a few weeks and then put her on the bottle which Anna took to well and Mrs. Martin's anxieties eased. By the time she was a year-old Anna was having milk from her bottle and some solid foods but without much enthusiasm. Here is a typical feed, when Anna was 13 months:

Anna sat in her highchair, watching her mother preparing her food. At first Mother offered Anna a cup of orange juice and she took a little. A bottle of water was then offered and energetically pushed away after a few sucks. Mother then offered her a small bottle of milk; Anna took it eagerly, put her head back and drank it all, gazing with a glazed expression at the ceiling. Mrs. Martin then offered Anna some cereal from a spoon. Anna took a few spoonfuls then reared up, arching her back and pulling away from the proffered spoon. She went stiff and then struggled to get out of her highchair. Mrs. Martin tried a few more times to no avail, then said, "All right, I won't force you," and lifted her out of the chair. She put on some music which Anna, waving her arms and listening, clearly liked. After a while Mrs. Martin picked her up and put her back in her highchair with Anna becoming more and more frantic as she was strapped in. She was momentarily distracted by a lid with a little knob on it which her mother put on the tray, and Mother was able to get a few spoonfuls into her mouth. However Anna soon resisted the spoon in the same way as before, until Mother gave up the attempt.

Anna shows in this feed how ambivalent she is towards the solid food from the spoon, and how attached she is to her bottle when she seems to go into a world of her own, away from her mother. Mrs. Martin seems at first to be able to accept Anna's vigorous refusal, but then her own anxieties about whether she has given Anna enough seem to emerge again and she cannot resist trying to get some more food into her. Anna complies for a while but then resists again, forcing Mother to give up. This kind of battle of wills, which many mothers experience with their toddlers, seems in danger of escalating between Anna and her mother into something very serious. With the benefit of hindsight, is there some way of thinking about the situation which would prevent such an escalation and help Anna to accept the solid food? She seems in fact to be very peaceful when she is watching her mother preparing the food. Perhaps if Mrs. Martin had put some kind of finger food on the tray at this point, Anna would have felt more able to take it or leave it of her own volition, spurred on by her hunger; or Mrs. Martin might have put the plate of cereal on the tray, leaving Anna to explore it before she ate, while Mother prepared the bottle. This of course means

Mother may have to tolerate some mess and face the possibility that the child is not interested in the food, in which case it may be better, after a few attempts at offering it on a spoon, to take it away altogether. The important thing would seem to be to allow the baby to feel that the solid food is something she has some control over, not something that is going to be forced down her throat. Anna's attachment to her bottle, seems to contain an element of rejection of her mother, and this was very hard for Mrs. Martin to bear. Anna did not even like her mother holding her while she drank her bottle. Sometimes the evident physical pleasure that a baby gets from sucking the bottle, as Anna clearly does in the above description (or from the breast for that matter), is disturbing to the mother and I think arouses worries that the baby will never give it up.

The feeding situation with Anna did become very tense indeed. Mrs. Martin would try to distract the baby with a whole gamut of toys while she sneaked the spoon into her mouth. In fact this was only partially successful as Anna became more and more wary, and then resistant to anything offered on a spoon. On one occasion, Mrs. Martin became so exasperated that she plonked the plate down on the tray saying, "Oh well, feed yourself then," and walked away; Anna then very tentatively dipped her fingers into the food and sucked it off! Mrs. Martin's worries about whether Anna was getting enough to eat made her offer big quantities of food which if she succeeded in getting into Anna, would be brought up later, or worse, during the night. On one occasion, Anna had been persuaded to eat a sizable amount of scrambled egg, and was then offered mashed banana and yogurt, both of which, not surprisingly, were refused adamantly. As adults, we know that having a huge meal put in front of us when we are not hungry can arouse feelings akin to panic; the same is true for a baby who is feeling picky or off-color when a large amount of food may in itself arouse the child's anxiety. Sometimes it does no harm for a baby to go away from a meal feeling a little hungry—she may even be more inclined to eat next time round.

Control and discipline

Our one year-old is now striking out on his own—taking the first steps towards separateness and autonomy. One of the first words he is likely to learn is "no"—essential for him in his struggle to become an individual with a sense of identity and ideas of his own. In order to progress and learn to do things for himself he must resist his parents' wishes to do things for him. This may mean developing in a different way from what his parents anticipated or wanted. As with food, it is usually counter-productive to try to force a child into a mold, or into being something he is not. For example trying to make a boy who is by nature quiet or shy into a boisterous extrovert may well have the opposite effect and make him feel anxious that his natural way of being is not acceptable to his parents.

Letting your baby say no

It is terribly important that a child is given the time and opportunity to find out for himself what his capacities and resources are. This means listening to him, and as far as is possible, taking his "no's" seriously. If his natural inclination to say no at this stage is never respected, he may become either over-obedient because he also desperately needs his parents' love and approval, or excessively contrary and obstinate. Most parents, if asked, would agree that they would want their child to grow up having a mind of his own, not slavishly conforming to what other people want of him. Saying no inevitably contains aggression and rejection and at this crucial stage the baby needs to have some experience of being able to express these feelings without being punished or made to feel he is just being naughty. If the baby has a general feeling of being respected and listened to when he wants to do things for himself in his own time he is more likely to co-operate when it is necessary for him to be hurried along. Similarly, if he is given reasonable freedom to explore and test things out, he will more readily submit to rules and prohibitions when it is important that he should.

Discipline and punishment

Parents of toddlers often get into difficulties over how to discipline their child or, sometimes, whether to discipline them at all, the fear being that discipline will inhibit natural growth and free expression. Discipline, in my view, is by no means the same as punishment, which usually means inflicting physical pain or some kind of deprivation on the child. All parents, at one time or another are likely to mete out some kind of punishment, like a slap in a moment of exasperation. If such punishment is the exception rather than the rule the child will probably recognize it correctly as meaning that she has gone too far this time. It may even be salutary at times for the child to realize that parents' patience is not inexhaustible. It is unreasonable to expect oneself to be always understanding or always tolerant. On the other hand to be forever spanking a child will make her more rebellious, or worse, teach her that only physical strength matters. Parents tend to be over-severe in their dealings with their child when they see behavior which reminds them of something they feel touchy about in themselves or if the behavior reflects badly on them. A one year-old has very strong feelings and impulses which at times get the better of her and result in her doing things which make her feel frightened. On such occasions she needs to feel that there is a firm parent or adult around who will take control and put a stop to undesirable behavior without becoming too punitive.

This thorny issue of control and discipline frequently comes into focus when a new baby arrives, and the toddler is overcome with feelings of jealousy and hatred towards the newcomer. A too-tight hug, or a surreptitious punch or poke at the baby happen at moments when the toddler's feelings have become too much for him and he wants to hurt the baby. Some parents find it difficult to accept the notion that their child could harbor such negative and hateful feelings and try to turn a blind eye to them. In the long run this is not helpful because if the child is not stopped he gets frightened of what he can do and actually hurting the baby would make him feel very guilty. It is important for parents in such a situation not to punish the child but to recognize that such feelings are normal, to help the child control his feelings, and to take steps to prevent him doing any actual harm.

Parents need to be firm

Part of the business of parenting a one year-old is knowing when to set limits and say no. There are innumerable occasions when "no" is needed—for instance, when the child has had enough sweets for that day, or enough time playing in the bath. Confrontations at such moments are inevitable and the child's anger at being denied or thwarted has to be withstood. If the parents are on the whole in agreement about where the limits should be, these moments of conflict can usually be managed. A child will be very confused if his parents are at loggerheads over this—if one parent is very lenient leaving the other to be the baddie who is always dishing out the discipline. Not infrequently this results in the child playing one parent off against the other and becoming very manipulative. Sometimes it is good for a child to be able to get away with something, or to feel he can hoodwink his mom or dad. It is also important to be clear when it is a game and when it is really serious. A child of this age needs his parents to stop him from being destructive or riding roughshod over other members of the family.

Toilet training

Issues of control and discipline come into play with toilet training. On the whole it is not realistic to expect a baby to be consistently clean and dry before the end of the second year, often even later. Before this the baby is unlikely to have gained full sphincter control. More important he needs to be emotionally ready and willing to co-operate in the process. If he is forced too early he may seem to comply, only to lapse later on when he is struggling to gain more control over his body in other ways.

For small infants, the contents of their bodies are closely associated with good or bad feelings. A tummy full of warm milk, a mouth with a nipple in it to hang on to and suck; these things give him a good bodily feeling of a mother who is present and caring for him. A tummy full of gas, a full bladder or bowel give him feelings of pain and discomfort which he instinctively gets rid of by expelling them, thus getting back the good feeling. In this the baby has been encouraged by his mother who smiles and says, "that's good," and, "that's better," indicating that she is pleased with a full diaper or burps. After all, regular dirty diapers are a welcome indication that the baby is functioning well and thriving. As the infant grows he becomes more aware of the pleasure his messes give his mother and he comes to regard them as gifts for her.

During this second year as babies are struggling to establish their separateness, they come to view their feces and urine as their own possessions which they want to give up or hang on to in their way and in their own good time, and it is very important to recognize and respect such wishes in this regard. Sunni's mother noticed that around 15 months, she would take herself off to a quiet place, usually squeezing between a cupboard and a wall, where she would defecate into her diaper with great concentration, not allowing her mother anywhere near her. Only when she emerged from what her mother referred to with good humor, as "poo corner," would she permit her mother to clean her up. This went on for several months before she could be persuaded to put her feces into a potty.

Avoiding angry battles

Toilet training is more likely to be successful if the infant is allowed some control over the process. Most babies take a long time to be fully clean and dry with a great many accidents on the way, either genuine ones or on purpose. They will undoubtedly go through periods of just not wanting to conform, when their waste products can be used as secret weapons to defy mother. If the mother can tolerate her baby's moments of angry defiance over this issue, and capitalize on the constructive impulses to become more grown up, there is less likelihood of a battle of wills occurring. Encouragement to be more grown-up and put messes in the right place should follow the child's cues, and be done tactfully, as the baby has to come to realize that body wastes are, alas, just that, and not wondrous treasures, as they seemed to be when he was a small infant. If your baby is too abruptly given the message that he is dirty, he may feel crushed and humiliated and fears arouse that he is thought of as dirty.

Towards the end of the second year the baby will probably be indicating to his mother that he has a dirty diaper, perhaps by walking in an awkward way, by a particular look on his face, or like Sunni by going to a certain spot in the house. Your baby may by this stage have his own particular words for his feces and urine. The capacity to put a word to them is already a step towards gaining control. Having a potty around the house long before it will be used is helpful because the mother can begin to talk to the baby about the potty—show it to him, and explain what it is for. Later on she can explain where grown-ups like Daddy and Mommy put their messes, and suggest he might like to do the same. Once your baby has got the idea of using the potty he can be prepared for the later transition to the washroom by being allowed with Mother's help to put the contents down the toilet and flush it away.

Temper tantrums

We have seen how in this phase of her development, the baby feels pulled in two directions. Your baby has a natural urge to find her own way and gain more control over her world and what happens to her. To do this she has to differentiate herself from her mother and move away from her. The urge to progress and grow up is often at odds with another wish to stay in a safe and special baby relationship with her mother. During this stage your child feels more painfully aware of her smallness and vulnerability, when she needs her parents and realizes she cannot control things as she would like to. Sometimes this conflict becomes too much and her feelings burst out of her in an uncontrolled way and she has a tantrum.

Temper tantrums are a mixture of rage and frustration; when such feelings become too much to bear he can only get rid of them in a violent way, much as he did when he was an infant and he expelled bad feelings from his bottom or through screaming. Being with a child having a full-blown tantrum is an unnerving experience for a parent. The child also may be frightened that the sheer violence of his feelings will harm him or his mother. If the tantrum happens in a public place, as seems so often embarrassingly to be the case, it helps both the child and the parent to haul the child off to some quiet spot where he can be physically held until he calms down. Then you can begin to try to sort out what might have triggered it. One mother reported that when her toddler had a tantrum at home she would put her in a corner. She seemed to be acknowledging that she was having difficulty controlling her own anger with the child and was using the two walls to hold her little girl together. Some children are better left alone and don't want mother anywhere near when they are having a tantrum. They will then spontaneously recover and gather themselves together; it may also be necessary for Mother to have the chance to cool off. It is then very important to try and get back to some kind of loving feelings with the child, and perhaps to talk about it later in simple language to see what it was all about.

Temper tantrums to some extent are part and parcel of the process of growing up and have to be weathered. If they are happening a lot the parents may need to ask themselves if they are constraining the child too much, or if they are expecting too high standards of behavior. If a child is given too much freedom without the security of knowing his parents can set limits when necessary he may feel under pressure to cope with more than he can manage at this stage in his development.

Fears

Children of this age are liable to develop all sorts of fears, sometimes in a mild way, sometimes strongly. These often seem very irrational and it is very perplexing when reassurance and explanations do not seem to help. A common fear is of loud noises, such as the sound of a vacuum cleaner, or the toilet flushing. Sometimes fears like these will pass as the child becomes familiar with them. If the fear persists it is very important not to expose the child deliberately to the source of the fear in the hope that he will be cured of it in this way—such tactics will only succeed in making him more terrified.

Understanding where these fears come from is difficult as they often appear suddenly and for no apparent reason, as though coming from something inside the child. Even when it is clear to an adult that there is nothing to be frightened of, it is important to accept that to the child, there is a real basis for his fear. The baby, as we have seen with the temper tantrums, has very strong feelings, some warm and loving, some angry and destructive, and he has all these in relation to his mother, still the central figure in his life and recipient of all his emotions. When his angry and destructive feelings are uppermost he fears that they will be harmful to his mother, and also that she will in turn retaliate and feel angry and hostile towards him. Sudden and inexplicable fears could then be understood as actually coming from his own destructive feelings which he disowns and attributes say, to the toilet noise which might suck him down as well as his feces, or to the teeth of a dog which may bite him. It is helpful to remember that in general such fears pass.

In this chapter we have seen some of the anxieties and concerns that most parents come up against at this stage in their child's life. Bringing up children is hard physical and emotional work, needing skill, patience and sometimes sheer staying power! It feels impossible to believe, in the lonely hours of the morning with a screaming baby, or when frantic with worry about loss of appetite, or driven to the limits of exasperation when he is just being plain contrary, that your child will eventually reach adulthood, relatively unscathed. Talking to one's partner, or a close friend, can be a life-saver at these times and will help to restore a sense of perspective and maybe a sense of humor. Talking to the parents of older children can be really helpful, as they undoubtedly will have gone through some similar experiences. All kinds of mother-toddler groups are a godsend for the mother as well as the baby; looking after a small child can be a very isolating job, especially for single parents. Having a supportive network around her will enable the mother to recharge her batteries from time to time and to take time off to enjoy this delightful, exhilarating, but never-to-be-recaptured period of her child's life.

CHAPTER FOUR

Play

Why do children play? An obvious answer, but one worth stating nevertheless, is because they enjoy it; they enjoy the physical and emotional experience of play and the opportunity to explore their surroundings. For the small child whose verbal skills are limited, play is also a way of expressing his inner feelings and experience. Playing is as vital to a child's well being as eating and sleeping.

Providing toys and materials for the small child to play with is important, but too many toys, apart from being very expensive, can inhibit the child's learning to find objects for himself and inventing his own games with them. A safe environment in which to play is also important and now is the time to make the house as safe as possible and to remove precious items out of reach; doing this will save a lot of aggravation for parents and baby, and leave more energy to cope with really unavoidable conflicts between what the baby wants to do and what his mother and Father thinks it is safe for him to do.

In the second year of life, children through their play are beginning to learn about the outside world and how to manage it. They are also exploring the nature and extent of their own feelings and resources when they meet the outside world. They do this by manipulating and exploring the possibilities of the toys and of various household objects. They learn by watching and copying other children and adults. The lively one year-old is interested in everything, even seemingly trivial things which have long lost their fascination for adults. There is something very moving about the intense seriousness with which the one year-old sets about his discoveries; A. A. Milne in his Winnie-the-Pooh books captured something of this touching quality with great humor, as in his story of Eeyore's Birthday, when Pooh gives him an empty honey jar (having been unable to resist eating the honey) and Piglet gives him a balloon (which he has accidentally fallen on and burst).

When Eeyore saw the Pot, he became very excited. "Why," he said, "I believe my balloon will just go into that Pot."

"Oh no Eeyore," said Pooh, "balloons are much too big to go into Pots. What you do with a balloon is, you hold the balloon..."

"Not mine," said Eeyore proudly, "Look, Piglet." And as Piglet looked sorrowfully around, Eeyore picked the balloon up with his teeth, and placed it carefully in the pot; picked it out and put it on the ground; and then picked it up again and put it carefully back.

"So it does," said Pooh. "It goes in."

"So it does," said Piglet. "And it comes out."

"Doesn't it?" said Eeyore. "It goes in and out like anything."

"I'm very glad," said Pooh happily, "that I thought of giving you a Useful Pot to put things in."

"I'm very glad," said Piglet happily, "that I thought of giving you

Something to put in a Useful Pot."

But Eeyore wasn't listening. He was taking the balloon out, and putting it back again, as happy as could be...

Given the freedom and opportunity, children of this age have an infinite capacity to make an interesting activity out of ordinary objects—a capacity which we as adults have lost. Perhaps it is this that makes watching them intent on their play so appealing. There is something about their close involvement in what might seem to an adult to be a very small activity, which conveys the feeling that playing is not just enjoyable but is a very serious business.

Providing for play

At the end of the first year and beginning of the second, the baby will be happy with toys that he can bang, push, pull, prod, squeeze; he will enjoy saucepans, lids spoons; he may become fascinated by turns in handles, doorknobs, keys, shoes; all will no doubt be sucked, bitten, dropped, turned upside down, sat on, kicked. The possibilities are endless for your one year-old's insatiable curiosity. In doing all these things he is learning about the properties of things, how they work, what he can do with them, what they are for.

By 12 months many children have developed an interest in containers and things associated with them like lids and doors and handles. Many a child at this age will spend a long time, like Eeyore, putting things into things and often more important, dumping them out. Thus a shape box with may be used first of all in this way before the child becomes interested in the idea of putting the shapes through the right holes. An extension of this is her interest in cupboards, opening them and pulling things out. One child, Joey, developed a game which kept him amused for long periods. He would sit on the kitchen floor, pull all the pans and lids out and put them on top of the good-natured family dog lying on floor nearby. Every now and then the dog would get up tipping everything off and sending Joey into peals of laughter. Anna was fascinated by the cat-door. Having watched the cat go out, she would sit pushing the flap back and forth, looking through it and sometimes "posting" various objects through it.

Play as exploration

Putting things into things and tipping them out has such a widespread fascination for babies of this age that one is bound to surmise that it has a particular significance to them. We have seen how a small infant at the breast or bottle explores his mothers face, first with his eyes and later with his hands, patting her or putting his fingers in her mouth or nose. He has also been learning over the past months about his own body—poking his finger in his ear, playing with his toes, or his genitals as he sits in the bath. Both boys and girls will now be interested in the difference between their genitals and be curious about their different ways of urinating. So, when the baby drops his peas into his cup of orange juice or posts shapes into a saucepan he is not interested in doing things "correctly" but finding out what happens when different things come together, finding out about space, and about the relationship between different objects. Soon he will have endless fun finding out something similar with water in the bath or sink.

At this stage the physical explorations of the external world are closely associated with the baby's own bodily experiences and the child's mind also is beginning to be able to imagine what other people might be like. This development springs also from the inner experience of having a mother who was interested in what was going on inside them and how they might be feeling when they were infants. But a child of this age is only partly able to use his or her imagination in this way. A touching example of this was reported by one mother about her daughter, Gemma, who at 13 months saw her father looking upset one day. She was a child who, when she was upset, sucked her thumb and twisted a bit of her hair. When she saw her father's distress, she climbed on his knee and while sucking her own thumb tugged at a bit of his hair.

Many babies at around 12 months are very interested in watching grown-ups eating and drinking, and will often, for example want to feed Mother during mealtimes. Ryan would stand staring fixedly as his father sipped a drink—he seemed particularly fascinated by the Adam's apple going up and down!

Playing with your baby

Children at this age will often stand staring intently at what another child is doing or be embarrassingly uninhibited about watching curiously while another mother is dealing with her baby in the supermarket or on the bus. The toddler is interested in what is going on between them, identifying them with himself and his mother. Two-person games like, "where is Mommy's nose, where is Peter's nose?" and "Paddacakes" will be greatly enjoyed and with such games he is continually learning to differentiate between himself and another person and to find out who and what he is.

After several weeks of putting objects into containers and dumping them out again she will be more dexterous and will start learning to judge what objects will go into others and she will enjoy, for example, the sets of colored cups that fit inside each other. She will start to build up little towers of blocks, mainly for the much greater excitement of knocking them down. Playing at knocking things down or scattering things gives the child the opportunity to express her destructive feelings in a safe and controlled way. In the second half of this year the baby will be more interested in posting shapes into the right holes, or doing simple jigsaws. Completing a task like this gives the child a sense of order, and a sense of achievement and satisfaction about what she can do.

At this stage the baby needs mostly to be with or near his mother while he plays, so that he can refer back to her, show her what he is doing, gain her approval or elicit her help. It is a boon to a mother when her toddler can spend some time playing contentedly on his own while she is busy, and although children vary in how long they can sustain this, much of his capacity to entertain himself will come from his experience of being played with as an infant by a loving and interested mother. It is still very important for his future development, to take some time off to play with him, preferably taking cues from the child, following his lead, facilitating his play rather than taking it over.

Sometimes parents get impatient watching their baby doing something very ham-fistedly. There is a great temptation either to do it for him, or to show him how to do it better or more quickly. Constantly doing this, however, will undermine the child's confidence and prevent him or her gaining the experience of persevering and tolerating frustration. Mrs. Ramsey tended to do this when she played with her 13-month-old baby Theresa. A furry rabbit was put on a chair so that only the face was visible to Theresa. She was quick to see the chance of a game and crawled, smiling towards it, but before she could get to it her mother picked it up and gave it to her, saying, "There, give him a cuddle." Theresa showed her anger at being forestalled in this way by grabbing the rabbit, hugging it very hard indeed, then throwing it away. A few moments later, Theresa again showed very clearly how frustrated she was by her mother's over-eagerness. She was sitting by the baby walker which was full of blocks. After considerable effort, Theresa managed to pull out one of the blocks which she put on the floor. She was about to get another out when her mother quickly took out two or three more blocks and made a tower, at which Theresa flapped her hands and cried very loudly. Mrs. Ramsey instantly realized what she had done and she put the blocks back, saying "sorry" to her daughter.

The beginning of sociable play

It is not until the end of the second year that children begin to play together, but before they reach that stage they will benefit a great deal from being with other children of their own age, and playing alongside them. To begin with they will most likely stand and stare at one another, as though sizing each other up. Gradually they will start following each other around, copying each other and handing things back and forth. The chance to be with another child outside the family is invaluable as it provides the opportunity to explore another kind of relationship away from the cloistered and more intense atmosphere of his own family. Between children of different families there is not the same raw jealousy and competition for mother's attention.

Getting a child used to being with other children early on will not only help him with the beginnings of making social relationships but it will also make it easier for him to hold his own later in the inevitable bouts of toy-snatching. It is not realistic to expect children of this age to share toys—a hard lesson to learn—right now the baby is much more concerned with discovering what is his and what he can do with things.

Play as a way of coping

One of the most important functions of playing is that it helps the baby cope with all the complicated emotions of his life—love, hate, aggression, anxiety. As we have seen in preceding chapters, the baby feels all these things mainly in relation to his mother. Now he is more aware that the mother who feeds and comforts him and whom he loves, is the same mother who arouses his jealousy and aggression when she leaves him or thwarts him. One of the things Theresa did when she felt angry and frustrated with her mother was to hug her rabbit very hard and then throw it away violently. She was expressing towards the rabbit the conflicting feelings about her mother but in a safe way that did not actually hurt her mother.

Throwing toys away and getting them back again, or sometimes wanting someone else to get them, is sometimes the child's way of working through his anxieties about people going away and coming back. The immensely entertaining game of "peek-a-boo" which children of this age love serves the same function of enabling the child to play out and have some control over comings and goings in a way that he doesn't have when mother goes out, or puts him in his crib at night. Peter at 13 months was left in the care of his grandfather while his mother went shopping one afternoon. Just after his mother left Peter went and stood rather forlornly by the door where Mother had gone out. After a few minutes he went to his grandfather who took him on his knee. Peter found his grandfather's pen in his pocket and he developed a game where he dropped the pen through his grandfather's cupped hands, saying "gone" as it dropped to the floor. He laughed and bounced up and down as he picked it up and did it again. He seemed to be exploring and going over the idea of things being dropped and found, perhaps as he felt dropped when his mother went out.

The well-known English pediatrician and psychoanalyst Donald Winnicott once said that "there is always an element of anxiety in children's play." We saw how Peter managed his feelings of sadness that his mother had left by inventing a game. His play helped him to escape from the impact of a real situation which he found painful and beyond his control and his anxiety acted as a spur to activity. Zoe made up another sort of game which she played on one occasion when her mother had gone out shopping, leaving her with her father. After wandering around rather disconsolately for a while she went and got an old handbag of her mother's which she had been given to play with, draped it over her arm and trotted in and out of the living room door saying, "bye bye!" By playing at being the mommy who is leaving she was able to accept more easily the reality of being the little girl who had been left behind.

Stress and loss of the ability to play

Too much anxiety or stress can have the opposite effect and inhibit or disrupt imaginative play. Zoe's parents went away for a week, taking an older sister with them and leaving Zoe at home with her grandparents. Although in many ways Zoe coped very well with the long separation from her family, her play during this period became listless, as though she had run out of steam. For example, just before her parents had left she had learned to walk up the stairs by herself but during this week she reverted to crawling up. Similarly, she became uninterested in doing a jigsaw which she loved and could do; she merely put the pieces on top of the board, not in the right slots.

A friend of mother's reported on her behavior during this week: "Zoe lay quietly while her diaper was changed, not wriggling to get up as she usually did. She pointed to the window and said, "'ook," and the friend remembered how her mother would take her to the window to see the crane outside on a building site and Zoe would say "'ook," but now her tone was listless. When she was put on the floor she went and found a book which she tried to open at the bound edge and when she couldn't she began to pick bits of paper off the book and throw them around chuckling to herself. She then went and found her furry rabbit, showed it to the friend then threw it on the floor and she repeated this with a few other toys. She went and got two little cars and a little man out of her playhouse and wandered into the hall with them as though undecided what to do. She threw them on the floor. Then she picked up the little man and stuck her finger in the little hole at the bottom. She kept the man on her finger for a long time sucking it now and then.

After that she went and sat on the little rocking horse and rocked herself for a while. She indicated that she wanted to be lifted out and she then went back momentarily to the playhouse. She then returned to the rocking horse where she rocked herself again.

Zoe was normally an energetic, assertive little girl but in this episode she seems to be showing how much of a strain she is under. She can comfort herself a little with the "'ook" memory of mother and sucking the little man on her finger. When she goes back to the playhouse it looks as though she might be able to play again but she then returns to the comfort of rocking herself on the rocking horse.

Play and growing up

As the year progresses the baby's play becomes more imaginative, exploring for example the possibility of doing the things that he sees his mother or father do. Both boys and girls of this age play at being Mother feeding or cleaning up their dolls. They are trying out being somebody else and enjoying not being the dependent baby, for a change. Kate, aged 18 months became very interested in keys, so much so that after a while, the set of plastic keys did not satisfy her—she wanted the real thing, and a set of old keys was found for her. She would experiment about where she could put them, trying them in locks or holes and carrying them around with her. On one occasion they were found in one of the saucepans in the kitchen cupboard. She was, around this time very attached to her father and greeted his return at night with great delight. It seemed as though she was wanting very much to be like her father, whose return was signaled by the sound of the key in the front door. Kate would also watch with intense interest as her mother put the key in the ignition of the car and switched on the engine. It was also, perhaps, her way of expressing her longing to have some control over the comings and goings of her parents.

By the end of this year your child will be more able to play with other children and it is very important that he or she should have plenty of opportunity to do so. He will begin to create make-believe games in which he will take on different roles, make rules and take turns. Having the chance to be with other children now will greatly enhance his ability to hold his own later in the rough and tumble of daycare or nursery school.

In the course of this second year of life the baby has grown from an infant with a limited concept of the world to a toddler eager to thrust out into life. The two year-old's emotional and intellectual life have expanded and your child now seems to be a complete person ready to tackle the wider world.

FURTHER READING

The Making and Breaking of Affectional Bonds, John Bowlby, Tavistock Publications, 1979 Through the Night, Dilys Daws, London Free Association Books, 1989

Thinking about Parents and Young Children, Martha Harris, Clunie Press, 1975

The Diary of a Baby, Daniel Stern, New York Basic Books, 1990

The Child, the Family and the Outside World, D. W. Winnicott, Penguin Books, 1964

The Author

After completing a language degree at London University, Deborah Steiner worked part-time as a primary school teacher and wrote for BBC Radio Schools and ITV Children's Television. She trained as a Child Psychotherapist at the Tavistock Clinic and now works as a Senior Child Psychotherapist at Enfield Child and Family Service. She is on the visiting staff of the Tavistock Clinic. She trained as a psycho-analyst at the Institute of Psychoanalysis and works in private practice as an analyst. She is married with three children. Publications include "The Internal Family and The Facts of Life," *Journal of Psycho-analytic Psychotherapy* (1989) Vol 4 No 1.

Understanding Your Child
Titles in This Series

Understanding Your Baby	by Lisa Miller
Understanding Your 1 Year-Old	by Deborah Steiner
Understanding Your 2 Year-Old	by Susan Reid
Understanding Your 3 Year-Old	by Judith Trowell
Understanding Your 4 Year-Old	by Lisa Miller
Understanding Your 5 Year-Old	by Lesley Holditch
Understanding Your 6 Year-Old	by Deborah Steiner
Understanding Your 7 Year-Old	by Elsie Osborne
Understanding Your 8 Year-Old	by Lisa Miller
Understanding Your 9 Year-Old	by Dora Lush
Understanding Your 10 Year-Old	by Jonathan Bradley
Understanding Your 11 Year-Old	by Eileen Orford
Understanding Your 12-14 Year-Olds	by Margot Waddell
Understanding Your 15-17 Year-Olds	by Jonathan Bradley & Hélène Dubinsky
Understanding Your 18-20 Year-Olds	by Gianna Williams
Understanding Your Handicapped Child	by Valerie Sinason